NATURAL HISTORY MUSEUMS, VOL. 1:

An Illustrated Guide to Over 350 Museums in the Eastern United States

**Compiled and Edited by
G. W. Bates**

Information on Vol. II,
Natural History Museums in the Western United States
may be obtained by writing the publisher:

**Batax Museum Publishing
301 Racquet Club Road, Suite 202
Fort Lauderdale, FL 33326**

The publisher of this guide makes no representation that it is absolutely accurate or complete. Errors and omissions, whether typographical, clerical or otherwise do sometimes occur and may occur anywhere within the body of this publication. The publisher does not assume and hereby disclaims any liability to any party for any loss or damage by errors or omissions resulting from negligence, accident or any other cause.

Library of Congress Cataloging-in-Publication Data

Bates, G. W., 1955-
    Natural history museums / compiled and edited by G.W. Bates.
      p. cm.
    Includes bibliographical references and index.
    Contents: v. 1. An illustrated guide to over 350 museums in the eastern United States
    ISBN 0-9629759-5-8 (v. 1) : $12.95
    1. Natural history museums—United States—Directories.
  I. Title.
  QH70.U6B38 1992
  508'.074'73-dc20   91-31840
                                        CIP

ATTENTION UNIVERSITIES, COLLEGES, AND PROFESSIONAL ORGANIZATIONS: Quantity discounts are available on bulk purchases of this book for educational purposes or fund raising. Special books or book excerpts can also be created to fit specific needs. For information, please contact Erma Torsiello, Batax Museum Publishing, 301 Racquet Club Road, Suite 202, Ft. Lauderdale, FL 33326, or call (305) 389-7033.

DEDICATION

This book is dedicated to my son Braedan.
Dad

ACKNOWLEDGMENT

I would like to thank the staff of the Broward County Libraries in Fort Lauderdale, Florida, that assisted me with reference material that helped make this book possible.

TABLE
OF CONTENTS

A star (★) next to a museum listing indicates that the museum refers to itself specifically as a Natural History Museum.

INTRODUCTION

The purpose of this guide is to provide you with a basic listing for museums containing a natural history collection. I have also listed some ideas to help make your museum visits more educational and enjoyable.

It's my objective to provide the most accurate and up-to-date list of natural history museums in the Eastern United States. The size and quality of a museum has not been important. The job has been to list museums, not to assess or grade them. Upon completion, my list totalled 358 museums. Unfortunately, it is impossible to list every facility of this type.

Some collections are located in historic homes; others are housed in multi-million dollar complexes complete with restaurants, theaters, concert halls, and gift shops. Generally, they are "user friendly," offering exhibits exciting to everyone.

Museums are constantly growing and changing. Artifacts and exhibits are often loaned to other museums. Some are placed in storage or, at times, are removed for scientific study. For this reason it is suggested you telephone just before your visit (phone numbers have been included) to check admission prices, hours, and accessibility. Special rates for group tours can usually be arranged.

For easy reference the museums are listed alphabetically by states, then cities, and finally by museum name. This East Coast volume, which represents 25 states and the District of Columbia, is illustrated with 26 photographs.

For explanation purposes, a natural history museum shall be recognized as any permanent institution which conserves and displays collections of objects of cultural or scientific significance for purpose of study, education, and enjoyment with at least a portion of the collection dedicated to natural history. Whether you are a collector, hobbyist, armchair naturalist, or simply planning to travel on vacation or business, these natural history museums are ready to welcome you.

72 IDEAS TO ENHANCE YOUR MUSEUM VISITS

1. Wear comfortable clothes, especially shoes.

2. Make note of rest room locations before you start.

3. Take a minute to get an overview of the museum using the map posted at the entrance or a brochure from the front desk.

4. If you have the time, prepare yourself with the "official museum guidebook" when available.

5. Make a list of exhibits you don't want to miss.

6. Be careful not to overplan. Be prepared for the element of surprise.

7. For a change, begin your tour randomly and don't worry about viewing in any particular sequence.

8. Check at the information desk to find out if there are any special activities for that day.

9. Stop at the gift shop before your visit. You could get some ideas of what to look for.

10. Try not to be too concerned about how much time you spend at each case. An exhibit can be appreciated in seconds—or longer periods can be spent on details not seen at first glance.

11. It is okay to be discriminating. View what you enjoy and avoid what you don't.

12. Read the labels for exhibits that appeal most to you on "this" visit.

13. Visit a museum with a friend and exchange thoughts. Four eyes are better than two.

14. Remember that what you do not see is never more important than what you do see.

15. When pressed for time, go through the museum quickly just to get an idea of what is there.

16. On a return visit take the time to study the exhibits in more detail.

17. Follow your instincts. Stay for as long or short a time as you wish.

18. The way in which the exhibit is displayed will sometimes influence your reaction. Take time to notice the presentation.

19. Stop at the gift shop at the end of your visit. You might notice an excellent exhibit you previously missed.

20. There are limits to your endurance, so take breaks.

21. Try sitting in front of an exhibit you would enjoy looking at in more detail.

22. Visit the cafeteria or snack bar to refresh yourself.

23. Visit a museum alone. A private visit can sometimes provide a greater impact on your experience.

24. After viewing an exhibit, try closing your eyes and reconstruct in your mind what you saw.

25. Try sketching an exhibit, even if you lack artistic ability. Your pencil will help you focus on detail you might otherwise miss.

26. Take advantage of guided tours, when available.

27. Ask questions when you would like to know more.

28. Prior knowledge about a museum or some of its exhibits will enrich your experience. Try to learn something before you go.

29. View an exhibit through a camera or opera glasses. This will help you "concentrate" and frame detail you might otherwise overlook.

30. Take some photographs to remember your visit.

31. When popular exhibits are too crowded, try viewing them just prior to closing or during lunch.

32. Use your imagination and put yourself in a make-believe situation with the exhibit.

33. Try to imagine what dinosaur bones would look like if they were covered with skin.

34. Pick out as many details of an exhibit as you can.

35. Visit some of the other facilities that many museums offer, such as libraries.

36. When available, take advantage of slide and video presentations. They can be a great help to your understanding and appreciation of an exhibit.

37. Visit the museum theater for special presentations.

38. Some museums offer behind-the-scene tours. Go on one when possible.

39. Try viewing with a taped pre-recorded tour.

40. Take part in a hands-on exhibit when possible.

41. Make a note of exhibits that leave lasting impressions. Make an effort to learn more about them and their background.

42. Take the time to see a "special" or "traveling" exhibition.

43. Learn to "see" rather than just "look." There *is* a difference.

44. Try to appreciate the enormous efforts that go into the making of these fine exhibits.

45. Ask yourself: what was the first thing you noticed in any particular exhibit? Why?

46. Try counting the number of animals in a diorama scene.

47. Take notice of the many different kinds of animals.

48. Look at the different colors in the scene.

49. Ask yourself: what time of day do you think the scene might be?

50. What season is it?

51. Do these animals have anything in common?

52. Try imagining the smell of the scene and what sounds the animals might be making.

53. Do the animals' facial expressions tell you anything?

54. How many different food sources can you find?

55. Try to imagine some appropriate background music for a diorama scene.

56. Is the scene a place that you would like to visit?

57. Try to identify yourself with any of the animals in a scene.

58. Look at a scene; then turn your back and try sketching what you remember.

59. Quiz yourself on why you think certain animals, like dinosaurs, became extinct.

60. Reflect on the field preparation used in the exhibit.

61. While observing, ask if you would add or delete anything in the scene.

62. Locate the largest object—and the smallest.

63. Use one word to describe any particular exhibit you wish.

64. Explain what you like or dislike in a diorama scene.

65. Use any available printed materials.

66. Try guessing the approximate ages, weights, and lengths of some dinosaurs. Check your answer with the label when possible.

67. View an exhibit from different angles, distances, and heights—such as kneeling down.

68. Spend a few moments reflecting on your visit.

69. Ask yourself: "How did the museum make me feel?"

70. Think back to the best exhibit you saw.

71. Figure out why that one created such a strong impression on you.

72. Try leaving the museum with a few images imprinted in your brain and your visit will truly have been a success.

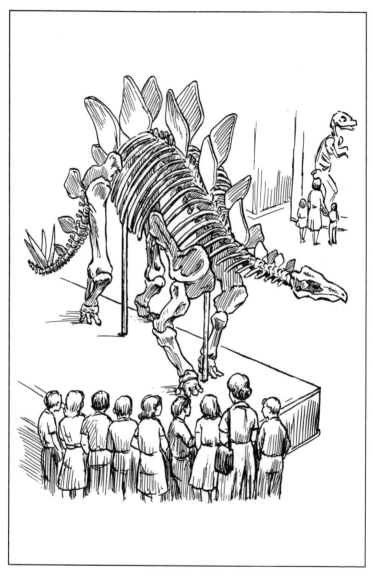

MUSEUMS are your passport to knowledge, entertainment, and fantasy.

THE MUSEUMS,
PART I

ALABAMA

★ **Anniston Museum of Natural History**
4301 McClellan Blvd.
Anniston, AL 36202
(205) 237-6766, Founded 1930.

The Discovery Place
of Birmingham, Inc.
1320 22nd St. South
Birmingham, AL 35205
(205) 939-1176, Founded 1981.

★ **Red Mountain Museum**
1421 22nd St. South
Birmingham, AL 35205
(205) 933-4152, Founded 1971.

Landmark Park
Highway 431 North
Dothan, AL 36302
(205) 794-3452, Founded 1976.

★ **Exploreum**
1906 Springhill Ave.
Mobile, AL 36607
(205) 471-5923, Founded 1979.

★ **The University of Alabama State Museum**
of Natural History
Smith Hall
University of Alabama
Tuscaloosa, AL 35487-0340
(205) 348-7550, Founded 1831.

George Washington Carver Museum
1212 Old Montgomery Rd.
Tuskegee Institute, AL 36088
(205) 727-6390, Founded 1941.

"Duck-billed" skeleton from the Cretaceous period.

CONNECTICUT

★ **Connecticut Audubon Society**
2325 Burr St.
Fairfield, CT 06430
(203) 259-6305, Founded 1898.

Goshen Historical Society
Old Middle Rd.
Goshen, CT 06756
(203) 491-2665, Founded 1955.

The Bruce Museum
Museum Drive
Greenwich, CT 06830
(203) 869-0376, Founded 1909.

Hungerford Outdoor Education Center
191 Farmington Ave.
Kensington, CT 06037
(203) 827-9064, Founded 1984.

White Memorial Conservation Center, Inc.
South of Route 202
Litchfield, CT 06759
(203) 567-0015, Founded 1964.

Lutz Children's Museum
247 S. Main St.
Manchester, CT 06040
(203) 643-0949, Founded 1953.

Mystic Marinelife Aquarium
55 Coogan Blvd.
Mystic, CT 06355-1997
(203) 536-9631, Founded 1973.

New Canaan Nature Center
144 Oenoke Ridge
New Canaan, CT 06840
(203) 966-9577, Founded 1960.

Hidden Valley Nature Center
Gillotti Road
New Fairfield, CT 06812
(203) 746-3095, Founded 1960.

★ **Peabody Museum of Natural History**
Yale University
170 Whitney Ave.
New Haven, CT 06511-8161
(203) 432-3750, Founded 1866.

Thames Science Center, Inc.
Gallows Lane
New London, CT 06320
(203) 442-0391, Founded 1948.

★ **Stamford Museum and Nature Center**
39 Scofieldtown Rd.
Stamford, CT 06903
(203) 322-1646, Founded 1936.

★ **The Connecticut State Museum
of Natural History**
75 N. Eagleville Rd., Room 312
Storrs, CT 06269-3023
(203) 486-4460, Founded 1982.

Science Museum of Connecticut
950 Trout Brook Dr.
West Hartford, CT 06119
(203) 236-2961, Founded 1927.

★ **Nature Center for Environmental Activities, Inc.**
10 Woodside Lane
Westport, CT 06880
(203) 227-7253, Founded 1958.

DELAWARE

Delaware Nature Society
Brackenville and Barley Mill Roads
Hockessin, DE 19707
(302) 239-2334, Founded 1964.

★ **Delaware Museum of Natural History**
4840 Kennett Pike
Wilmington, DE 19807
(302) 658-9111, Founded 1957.

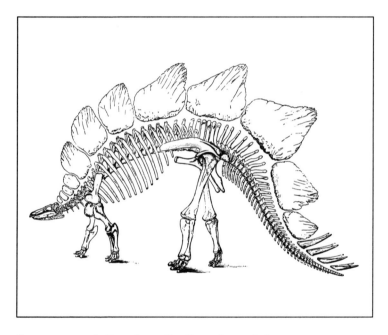

Stegosaurus skelton from the Jurassic period.

DISTRICT OF COLUMBIA

Explorers Hall
17th and M Streets NW
Washington, DC 20036
(202) 857-7000, Founded 1964.

★ **National Museum of Natural History**
10th St. and Constitution Ave. NW
Washington, DC 20560
(202) 357-1300, Founded 1846.

Rock Creek Nature Center
5200 Glover Rd. NW
Washington, DC 20015
(202) 426-6829, Founded 1960.

Smithsonian Institution
1000 Jefferson Dr.
Washington, DC 20560
(202) 357-1300, Founded 1846.

United States
Department of the Interior Museum
18th and C Streets NW
Washington, DC 20240
(202) 343-3477, Founded 1938.

FLORIDA

South Florida Museum and Bishop Planetarium
201 10th St. West
Bradenton, FL 34205
(813) 746-4131, Founded 1946.

Cedar Key State Museum
Off Highway 24 on Museum Drive
Cedar Key, FL 32625
(904) 543-5350, Founded 1962.

Brevard Museum, Inc.
2201 Michigan Ave.
Cocoa, FL 32926
(407) 632-1830, Founded 1969.

Museum of Arts and Sciences
1040 Museum Blvd.
Daytona Beach, FL 32014
(904) 255-0285, Founded 1971.

Discovery Center, Inc.
231 S.W. 2nd Ave.
Fort Lauderdale, FL 33301
(305) 462-4116, Founded 1976.

★ **Indian River Coastal Zone Museum**
5600 Old Dixie Highway
Fort Pierce, FL 34946
(407) 465-2400, Founded 1973.

★ **Florida Museum of Natural History**
University of Florida
Gainesville, FL 32611
(904) 392-1721, Founded 1917.

Gulf Islands National Seashore
1801 Gulf Breeze Pkwy.
Gulf Breeze, FL 32561
(904) 934-2600, Founded 1971.

Biscayne National Park
P.O. Box 1369
Homestead, FL 33090
(305) 247-2044, Founded 1968.

Everglades National Park
P.O. Box 279
Homestead, FL 33030
(305) 247-6211, Founded 1947.

Museum of Science and History, Jacksonville
1025 Gulf Life Dr.
Jacksonville, FL 32207
(904) 396-7062, Founded 1941.

East Martello Museum
3501 S. Roosevelt Blvd.
Key West, FL 33040
(305) 296-3913, Founded 1951.

Museum of Science
3280 S. Miami Ave.
Miami, FL 33129
(305) 854-4247, Founded 1949.

★ **Mulberry Phosphate Museum**
Highway 37 South
Mulberry, FL 33860
(813) 425-2823, Founded 1985.

Youth Museum of Charlotte County
260 W. Retta Esplanade
Punta Gorda, FL 33950
(813) 639-3777, Founded 1969.

★ **Safety Harbor Museum**
and Historical District
329 S. Bayshore Blvd.
Safety Harbor, FL 34695
(813) 726-1810, Founded 1977.

Washington Oaks State Gardens
Route 1, P.O. Box 128-A
St. Augustine, FL 32086
(904) 445-3161, Founded 1970.

The Science Center of Pinellas County
7701 22nd Ave. North
St. Petersburg, FL 33710
(813) 384-0027, Founded 1959.

★ **Fort Pickens Area-Gulf Islands**
National Seashore
1400 Fort Pickens Rd.
Santa Rosa Island, FL 32561
(904) 932-5307, Founded 1971.

Highlands Hammock State Park
Route 1, P.O. Box 310
Sebring, FL 33870
(813) 385-0011, Founded 1967.

★ **Tallahassee Junior Museum, Inc.**
3945 Museum Dr.
Tallahassee, FL 32310
(904) 576-1636, Founded 1957.

Museum of Science and Industry
4801 Fowler Ave.
Tampa, FL 33617-2099
(813) 985-5531, Founded 1962.

South Florida Science Museum
4801 Dreher Trail North
West Palm Beach, FL 33405
(407) 832-1988, Founded 1959.

Pioneer Park Museum
Highway and State Road 64
Zolfo Springs, FL 33890
(813) 735-0330, Founded 1966.

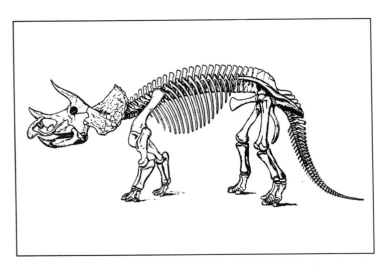

Triceratops skeleton from the late Cretaceous period.

GEORGIA

★ **University of Georgia Museum of Natural History**
Biological Science Building
University of Georgia
Athens, GA 30602
(404) 542-1663, Founded 1977.

Fernbank Science Center
156 Heaton Park Dr. NE
Atlanta, GA 30307
(404) 378-4311, Founded 1967.

Georgia State Museum of Science and Industry
Room 432
Georgia State Capitol
Atlanta, GA 30334
(404) 656-2846, Founded 1895.

Brasstown Bald Visitor Center
Highway 19 and 129 South
Blairsville, GA 30512
(404) 745-6928, Founded 1967.

★ **Lanier Museum of Natural History**
2601 Buford Dam Rd.
Buford, GA 30518
(404) 945-3543, Founded 1978.

Stephen C. Foster State Park
Route 1
Fargo, GA 31631
(912) 637-5274, Founded 1954.

Providence Canyon State Park
Route 1, P.O. Box 158
Lumpkin, GA 31815
(912) 838-6202, Founded 1971.

Museum of Arts and Sciences
4182 Forsyth Rd.
Macon, GA 31210
(912) 477-3232, Founded 1956.

Kiah Museum-A Museum for the Masses
505 W. 36th St.
Savannah, GA 31401
(912) 236-8544, Founded 1959.

Oatland Island Education Center
711 Sandtown Rd.
Savannah, GA 31410
(912) 897-3773, Founded 1974.

Savannah Science Museum, Inc.
4405 Paulsen St.
Savannah, GA 31405
(912) 355-6705, Founded 1954.

Georgia Southern Museum
P.O. Box 8061, Rosenwald Building
Statesboro, GA 30460
(912) 681-5444, Founded 1980.

ILLINOIS

University Museum
Southern Illinois University
Carbondale, IL 62901
(618) 453-5388, Founded 1869.

★ **Field Museum of Natural History**
Roosevelt Road at Lake Shore Drive
Chicago, IL 60605
(312) 922-9410, Founded 1893.

★ **Museum of the Chicago Academy of Sciences**
2001 N. Clark St.
Chicago, IL 60614
(312) 549-0606, Founded 1857.

Vermilion County Museum Society
116 N. Gilbert St.
Danville, IL 61832
(217) 442-2922, Founded 1964.

★ **Elgin Public Museum**
225 Grand Blvd.
Elgin, IL 60120
(708) 741-6655, Founded 1904.

Lizzadro Museum of Lapidary Art
220 Cottage Hill Ave.
Elmhurst, IL 60126
(708) 833-1616, Founded 1962.

Byer Museum of the Arts
1600 Orrington Ave.
Evanston, IL 60201
(708) 866-6600, Founded 1981.

Evanston Environmental Association
2024 McCormick Blvd.
Evanston, IL 60201
(708) 864-5181, Founded 1975.

**Kane County Forest Preserve
and Fabyan Villa**
1511 S. Batavia Ave.
Geneva, IL 60134
(708) 232-4811, Founded 1941.

★ **The Grove**
1421 Milwaukee Ave.
Glenview, IL 60025
(708) 299-6096, Founded 1976.

Dickson Mounds Museum
Lewistown, IL 61542
(309) 547-3721, Founded 1927.

★ **Jurica Natural History Museum**
Illinois Benedictine College
5700 College Rd.
Lisle, IL 60532
(708) 960-1500, Founded 1970.

Edgar County Historical Museum
414 N. Main
Paris, IL 61944
(217) 463-4580, Founded 1971.

★ **Quincy Museum of Natural History and Art**
1601 Maine St.
Quincy, IL 62301
(217) 224-7669, Founded 1966.

Fryxell Geology Museum
New Science Building
Augustana College
Rock Island, IL 61201
(309) 794-7318, Founded 1929.

★ **Burpee Museum of Natural History**
813 N. Main St.
Rockford, IL 61103
(815) 965-3132, Founded 1942.

★ **Spring Valley Nature Sanctuary**
1111 E. Schaumburg Rd.
Schaumburg, IL 60194
(708) 980-2100, Founded 1983.

★ **Illinois State Museum**
Spring and Edwards Streets
Springfield, IL 62706
(217) 782-7386, Founded 1877.

★ **Museum of Natural History,**
University of Illinois
1301 W. Green St.
Urbana, IL 61801
(217) 333-2517, Founded 1870.

Iroquois County Historical Society Museum
Old Courthouse, 2nd and Cherry
Watseka, IL 60970
(815) 432-2215, Founded 1967.

INDIANA

Monroe County Historical Society Museum
202 E. 6th St.
Bloomington, IN 47408
(812) 332-2517, Founded 1980.

Whitley County Historical Museum
108 W. Jefferson
Columbia City, IN 46725
(219) 244-6372, Founded 1963.

Evansville Museum of Arts and Science
411 S.E. Riverside Dr.
Evansville, IN 47713
(812) 425-2406, Founded 1926.

Clinton County Museum
301 E. Clinton St.
Frankfort, IN 46041
(317) 659-2030, Founded 1980.

Upper Wabash Basin Regional Resource Center
2303 College Ave.
Huntington, IN 46750
(219) 356-6000, Founded 1975.

The Children's Museum
3000 N. Meridian St.
Indianapolis, IN 46208
(317) 921-4019, Founded 1925.

Indiana State Museum
202 N. Alabama St.
Indianapolis, IN 46204
(317) 232-1637, Founded 1869.

Cass County Historical Society
1004 E. Market St.
Logansport, IN 46947
(219) 753-3866, Founded 1907.

Hannah Lindahl Children's Museum
1402 S. Main St.
Mishawaka, IN 46544
(219) 258-3056, Founded 1946.

**Biology Department Teaching Museum
and Nature Center**
2000 University
Muncie, IN 47306
(317) 285-8820, Founded 1918.

Henry County Historical Society
606 S. 14th St.
New Castle, IN 47362
(317) 529-4028, Founded 1886.

Miami County Museum
51 N. Broadway
Peru, IN 46970
(317) 472-3901, Founded 1916.

Indiana Dunes National Lakeshore
1100 N. Mineral Springs Rd.
Porter, IN 46304
(219) 926-7561, Founded 1970.

★ **Joseph Moore Museum**
Earlham College
Richmond, IN 47374
(317) 983-1303, Founded 1887.

Historical Society Porter County
Old Jail Museum
Old Jail Building
153 Franklin St.
Valparaiso, IN 46383
(219) 465-3595, Founded 1916.

Michel Brouillet House and Museum
509 N. 1st St.
Vincennes, IN 47591
(812) 885-4173, Founded 1975.

Ceratosaurus skelton from the Jurassic period.

KENTUCKY

Behringer-Crawford Museum
1600 Montague Rd.
Devou Park
Covington, KY 41012
(606) 491-4003, Founded 1950.

Clyde E. Buckley Wildlife Sanctuary
1305 Germany Rd.
Frankfort, KY 40601
(606) 873-5711, Founded 1967.

John James Audubon Museum
Audubon State Park
Henderson, Ky 42420
(502) 826-2247, Founded 1938.

★ **American Saddle Horse**
Museum Association, Inc.
4093 Iron Works Pike
Lexington, KY 40511
(606) 259-2746, Founded 1962.

Transylvania Museum
300 N. Broadway
Lexington, KY 40508
(606) 233-8228, Founded 1882.

★ **Museum of History and Science**
727 W. Main St.
Louisville, KY 40202
(502) 561-6100, Founded 1872.

Mammoth Cave National Park
P.O. Box 28
Mammoth Cave, KY 42259
(502) 758-2251, Founded 1941.

Blue Licks Battlefield Museum
Blue Licks Battlefield Park
Mount Olivet, KY 41064
(606) 289-5507, Founded 1928.

Owensboro Area Museum
2829 S. Griffith Ave.
Owensboro, KY 42301
(502) 683-0296, Founded 1966.

Lincoln Homestead State Shrine
Rural Route 1
Springfield, KY 40069
(606) 336-7461, Founded 1936.

Big Bone Orientation Center and Diorama
3380 Beaver Rd.
Union, KY 41091
(606) 384-3522, Founded 1971.

MAINE

Maine State Museum
State House Complex
Augusta, ME 04333
(207) 289-2301, Founded 1836.

★ **The Natural History Museum**
College of the Atlantic
Bar Harbor, ME 04609
(207) 288-5015, Founded 1982.

★ **Nylander Museum**
393 Main St.
Caribou, ME 04736
(207) 493-4474, Founded 1938.

Stanwood Wildlife Sanctuary
Route 3, Bar Harbor Road
Ellsworth, ME 04605
(207) 667-8460, Founded 1959.

The Monhegan Museum
Monhegan, ME 04852
Founded 1960.

Children's Museum of Maine
746 Stevens Ave.
Portland, ME 04103
(207) 797-5483, Founded 1977.

State of Maine Marine Resources Laboratory
McKown Point
West Boothbay Harbor, ME 04575
(207) 633-5572, Founded 1905.

MARYLAND

★ **Cylburn Nature Museum**
Cylburn Mansion
4915 Greenspring Ave.
Baltimore, MD 21209
(301) 396-0180, Founded 1954.

★ **Audubon Naturalist Society**
8940 Jones Mill Rd.
Chevy Chase, MD 20815
(301) 652-9188, Founded 1897.

★ **Anne Arundel Natural History Museum**
Carrie Weedon Center
Galesville, MD 20765
(301) 224-5000, Founded 1972.

Historic St. Mary's City
Route 5
St. Mary's City, MD 20686
(301) 862-0990, Founded 1966.

Calvert Marine Museum
14200 Solomons Island Rd.
Solomons, MD 20688
(301) 326-2042, Founded 1969.

MASSACHUSETTS

The Bartlett Museum
270 Main St., P.O. Box 423
Amesbury, MA 01913
(508) 388-4528, Founded 1968.

Museum of Zoology
Department of Zoology
University of Massachusetts
Amherst, MA 01003
(413) 545-0457, Founded 1863.

★ ### The Pratt Museum
of Natural History
Amherst College
Amherst, MA 01002
(413) 542-2165, Founded 1821.

Children's Museum
Museum Wharf
300 Congress St.
Boston, MA 02210-1034
(617) 426-6500, Founded 1913.

Museum of Science
Science Park
Boston, MA 02114-1099
(617) 589-0100, Founded 1830.

★ ### Cape Cod Museum
of Natural History, Inc.
Route 6A
Brewster, MA 02631
(617) 896-3867, Founded 1954.

Museum of Comparative Zoology
26 Oxford St.
Cambridge, MA 02138
(617) 495-2463, Founded 1859.

**Arcadia Nature Center
and Wildlife Sanctuary**
127 Combs Rd.
Easthampton, MA 01027
(413) 584-3009, Founded 1944.

**Laughing Brook Education Center
and Wildlife Sanctuary**
789 Main St.
Hampden, MA 01036
(413) 566-8034, Founded 1966.

Pleasant Valley Trailside Museum
Pleasant Valley Wildlife Sanctuary
Lenox, MA 01240
(413) 637-0320, Founded 1950.

Drumlin Farm Education Center
Lincoln Road
Lincoln, MA 01773
(617) 259-9807, Founded 1954.

★ **Blue Hills Trailside Museum**
1904 Canton Ave.
Milton, MA 02186
(617) 333-0690, Founded 1959.

★ **Nantucket Maria Mitchell Association**
2 Vestal St.
Nantucket, MA 02554
(617) 228-9198, Founded 1902.

South Shore Natural Science Center, Inc.
Jacobs Lane
Norwell, MA 02061
(617) 659-2559, Founded 1962.

★ **The Berkshire Museum**
39 South St.
Pittsfield, MA 01201
(413) 443-7171, Founded 1903.

Peabody Museum of Salem
East India Square
Salem, MA 01970
(508) 745-1876, Founded 1799.

Thornton W. Burgess Museum
4 Water St.
Sandwich, MA 02563
(508) 888-4668, Founded 1976.

Children's Museum
276 Gulf Rd.
South Dartmouth, MA 02748
(617) 993-3361, Founded 1952.

The Skinner Museum
of Mount Holyoke College
35 Woodbridge St.
South Hadley, MA 01075
(413) 538-2085, Founded 1933.

Historical Natural History
and Library Society of Natick
Bacon Free Library Building–Eliot St.
South Natick, MA 01760
(617) 235-6015, Founded 1870.

Cape Cod National Seashore
South Wellfleet, MA 02663
(508) 349-3785, Founded 1961.

Springfield Science Museum
236 State St.
Springfield, MA 01103
(413) 733-1194, Founded 1859.

Aquarium of the National Marine Fisheries Service
Water Street
Woods Hole, MA 02543
(508) 548-7684, Founded 1885.

New England Science Center
222 Harrington Way
Worchester, MA 01604
(508) 791-9211, Founded 1971.

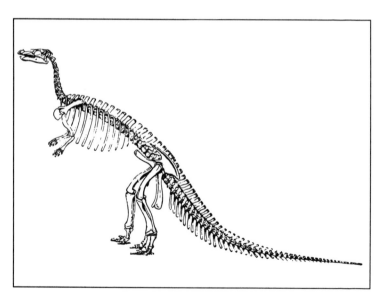

Camptosaurus skeleton from the Jurassic period.

MICHIGAN

The Ann Arbor Hands-On Museum
219 E. Huron St.
Ann Arbor, MI 48104
(313) 995-5437, Founded 1982.

★ **The University of Michigan-Exhibit Museum**
1109 Geddes Ave.
Ann Arbor, MI 48109-1079
(313) 763-4191, Founded 1817.

★ **Kingman Museum of Natural History**
West Michigan Avenue at 20th St.
Battle Creek, MI 49017
(616) 965-5117, Founded 1869.

Cranbrook Institute of Science
500 Lone Pine Rd., P.O. Box 801
Bloomfield Hills, MI 48013
(313) 645-3260, Founded 1930.

Belle Nature Center
Belle Isle Park
Detroit, MI 48207
(313) 267-7157, Founded 1976.

Detroit Science Center
5020 John R. St.
Detroit, MI 48202
(313) 577-8400, Founded 1970.

★ **The Wayne State University Museum
of Natural History**
637 Science Library, Wayne State University
Detroit, MI 48202
(313) 577-2886, Founded 1972.

The Michigan State University Museum
West Circle Drive
East Lansing, MI 48824
(517) 355-2370, Founded 1857.

Sloan Museum
1221 E. Kearsley St.
Flint, MI 48503
(313) 762-1170, Founded 1966.

★ **Call of the Wild Museum**
850 S. Wisconsin Ave.
Gaylord, MI 49735
(517) 732-4336, Founded 1957.

Public Museum of Grand Rapids
54 Jefferson SE
Grand Rapids, MI 49503
(616) 456-3977, Founded 1854.

De Graaf Nature Center
600 Graafschap Rd.
Holland, MI 49423
(616) 396-2739, Founded 1962.

Kalamazoo Nature Center, Inc.
7000 N. Westnedge Ave.
Kalamazoo, MI 49007-9711
(616) 381-1574, Founded 1960.

★ **Carl G. Fenner Arboretum
and Environmental Education Center**
2020 E. Mt. Hope Rd.
Lansing, MI 48910
(517) 483-4224, Founded 1959.

Woldumar Nature Center
5539 Lansing Rd.
Lansing, MI 48917
(517) 322-0030, Founded 1966.

Stuart House Museum
of Astors American Fur Co.
Trading Post
Market Street
Mackinac Island, MI 49757
(906) 847-3259, Founded 1810.

Mackinac State Historic Parks-Mill Creek
Mackinac City, MI 49701
(616) 436-7301, Founded 1975.

Chippewa Nature Center
400 S. Badour Rd., Route 9
Midland, MI 48640
(517) 631-0830, Founded 1966.

Kensington Metro Park Nature Center
2240 W. Buno Rd.
Milford, MI 48042
(313) 685-1561, Founded 1957.

Center for Cultural and Natural History
Bellows St., 124 Rowe Hall
Mount Pleasant, MI 48859
(517) 774-3829, Founded 1970.

Muskegon County Museum
430 W. Clay
Muskegon, MI 49440
(616) 722-0278, Founded 1937.

Fernwood Nature Center
and Botanical Gardens
13988 Rangeline Rd.
Niles, MI 49120
(616) 695-6491, Founded 1964.

Dinosaur Gardens, Inc.
11160 U.S. 23 South
Ossineke, MI 49766
(517) 471-5477, Founded 1934.

Museum of Arts and History
1115 Sixth St.
Port Huron, MI 48060
(313) 982-0891, Founded 1967.

Seney National Wildlife Refuge Visitor Center
Seney National Wildlife Refuge
Seney, MI 49883
(906) 586-9851, Founded 1963.

Great Lakes Area Paleontological Museum
381 S. Long Lake Rd.
Traverse City, MI 49684
(616) 943-8850, Founded 1971.

PHOTO
PORTFOLIO

Anniston Museum of Natural History
Anniston, Alabama

Photo courtesy of Anniston Museum of Natural History
Among the collection is this African Diorama.

Stamford Museum and Nature Center
Stamford, Connecticut

Photo courtesy of Stamford Museum and Nature Center
Farmers' Year Exhibit at the Heckscher Farm.

Delaware Museum of Natural History
Wilmington, Delaware

Photo courtesy of Delaware Museum of Natural History
The African water hole diorama.

National Museum of Natural History
Washington, D.C.

Photo courtesy of National Museum of Natural History
Rotunda of National Museum of Natural History.

Museum of Science
Miami, Florida

Photo by G.W. Bates
The informative Coral Reef Exhibit.

Museum of Arts and Sciences
Macon, Georgia

Photo courtesy of Museum of Arts and Sciences
Among the collection are local wildlife specimens.

Field Museum of Natural History
Chicago, Illinois

Photo by G.W. Bates
Carl E. Akeley's "Fighting Elephants" group.

Indiana State Museum
Indianapolis, Indiana

Photo courtesy of Indiana State Museum

Learn more about the Em-Roes by visiting the Indiana State Museum.

The American Saddle Horse Museum
Lexington, Kentucky

Photo courtesy of The American Saddle Horse Museum
Museum artifacts relating to the Saddlebred horse.

The Natural History Museum
Bar Harbor, Maine

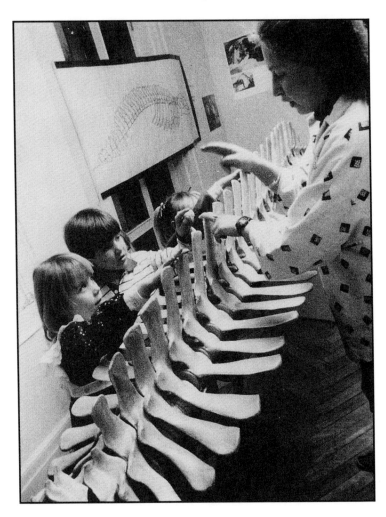

Photo courtesy of The Natural History Museum
The "Whale on Wheels" exhibit.

Calvert Marine Museum
Solomons, Maryland

Photo courtesy of Calvert Marine Museum
A popular exhibit, the Drum Point Lighthouse.

Cape Cod Museum of Natural History
Brewster, Massachusetts

Photo courtesy Cape Cod Museum of Natural History
This attraction includes three nature trails.

Detroit Science Center
Detroit, Michigan

Photo courtesy of Detroit Science Center

Also housed are the Discovery Theatre and Omnimax Space Theatre.

The Woodman Institute
Dover, New Hampshire

Garrison House, Over ... Years old Dover, N.H.

Photo courtesy of The Woodman Institute

Museum is housed in the 1675, Old Garrison House.

The Newark Museum
Newark, New Jersey

Photo Courtesy of The Newark Museum
This view shows the Newark Museum's new, three-story North Wing Atrium.

American Museum of Natural History
New York, New York

Photo courtesy of American Museum of Natural History
337292, Department of Library Services
Watercolor-View from West 77th Street, NY.

Schiele Museum of Natural History
Gastonia, North Carolina

Photo courtesy of Schiele Museum of Natural History
Take advantage of the museum's guided tours.

Cleveland Museum of Natural History
Cleveland, Ohio

Photo courtesy of Cleveland Museum of Natural History

Haplocanthosaurus delfsi, or "Happy", is mounted in Kirtland Hall.

Carnegie Museum of Natural History
Pittsburgh, Pennsylvania

Photo by G.W. Bates
Among the many dioramas is this bear exhibit.

Roger Williams Park Museum of Natural History
Providence, Rhode Island

Photo courtesy of Roger Williams Park Museum of Natural History

Also housed here is the Cormack Planetarium.

Museum of York County
Rock Hill, South Carolina

Photo courtesy of Museum of York County
An excellent display of the African elephant.

Memphis Pink Palace Museum and Planetarium
Memphis, Tennessee

Photo courtesy of Memphis Pink Palace Museum and Planetarium
Memphis Pink Palace Museum and Planetarium expansion
project, 1991.

Fairbanks Museum and Planetarium
St. Johnsbury, Vermont

Photo courtesy of Fairbanks Museum and Planetarium
This collection includes 2,600 mounted birds and mammals.

Virginia Museum of Natural History
Martinsville, Virginia

Photo courtesy of Virginia Museum of Natural History
Sloth Exhibit, "Sticks and Stones and Fossil Bones."

Sunrise Museums
Charleston, West Virginia

Photo courtesy of Sunrise Museums
Sunrise Museums from downtown historic Charleston.

Milwaukee Public Museum
Milwaukee, Wisconsin

Photo courtesy of Milwaukee Public Museum, # X-483-6H
3rd floor Rain Forest Exhibit.

THE MUSEUMS, PART II

NEW HAMPSHIRE

Audubon Society of New Hampshire
3 Silk Farm Rd.
Concord, NH 03301
(603) 224-9909, Founded 1914.

Annie E. Woodman Institute
182-192 Central Ave.
Dover, NH 03820
(603) 742-1038, Founded 1916.

★ **Science Center of New Hampshire**
Route 113
Holderness, NH 03245
(603) 968-7194, Founded 1966.

★ **Bear Brook Nature Center**
Bear Brook State Park
Suncook, NH 03275
(603) 485-3782, Founded 1961.

★ **Libby Museum**
Route 109 North
Wolfeboro, NH 03894
(603) 569-1035, Founded 1912.

NEW JERSEY

Allaire Village
Allaire State Park, Route 524
Allaire, NJ 07727
(201) 938-2253, Founded 1957.

**Environmental Education Center,
Somerset County Park Commission**
190 Lord Stirling Rd.
Basking Ridge, NJ 07920
(201) 766-2489, Founded 1970.

Hopewell Museum
28 E. Broad St.
Hopewell, NJ 08525
(609) 466-0103, Founded 1924.

Poricy Park Nature Center
Oak Hill Road
Middletown, NJ 07748
(201) 842-5966, Founded 1978.

The Morris Museum
6 Normandy Heights Rd.
Morristown, NJ 07960
(201) 538-0454, Founded 191?.

★ **Trailside Nature and Science Center**
Coles Avenue and New Providence Road
Mountainside, NJ 07092
(201) 789-3670, Founded 1941.

The Newark Museum
49 Washington St.
Newark, NJ 07101-0540
(201) 596-6550, Founded 1909.

Sussex County Historical Society
82 Main St.
Newton, NJ 07860
(201) 383-6010, Founded 1904.

Ocean City Historical Museum
1139 Wesley Ave.
Ocean City, NJ 08226
(609) 399-1801, Founded 1964.

Bergen Museum of Art and Science
Ridgewood Avenue and Fairview Avenue
Paramus, NJ 07652
(201) 265-1248, Founded 1956.

★ **Paterson Museum**
2 Market St.
Paterson, NJ 07501
(201) 881-3874, Founded 1925.

★ **Princeton University Museum
of Natural History**
Princeton University, Guyot Hall
Princeton, NJ 08544
(609) 452-4102, Founded 1805.

Meadowlands Museums
91 Crane Ave.
Rutherford, NJ 07070
(201) 935-1175, Founded 1961.

Cora Hartshorn Arboretum
324 Forest Dr. South
Short Hills, NJ 07078
(201) 376-3587, Founded 1960.

**Space Farms Zoological Park
and Museum**
Beemerville Road
Sussex, NJ 07461
(201) 875-5800, Founded 1927.

New Jersey State Museum
205 W. State St., CN 530
Trenton, NJ 08625-0530
(609) 292-6300, Founded 1895.

**James A. McFaul Wildlife Center
of Bergen County**
Crescent Avenue
Wyckoff, NJ 07481
(201) 891-5571, Founded 1967.

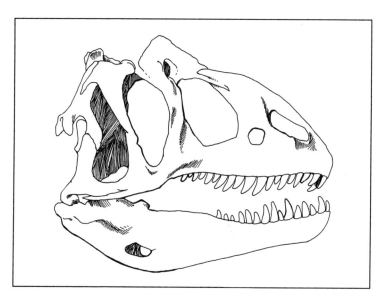

Skull of *Allosaurus*, meaning "different lizard."

NEW YORK

New York State Museum
Cultural Education Center
Empire State Plaza
Albany, NY 12230
(518) 474-5877, Founded 1870.

Walter Elwood Museum
300 Guy Park Ave.
Amsterdam, NY 12010
(518) 843-3180, Founded 1940.

★ **Bear Mountain Trailside Museums and Zoo**
Bear Mountain State Park
Bear Mountain, NY 10911
(914) 786-2701, Founded 1927.

Roberson Center for the Arts and Sciences
30 Front St.
Binghamton, NY 13905
(607) 772-0660, Founded 1954.

Northwind Undersea Institute
610 City Island Ave.
Bronx, NY 10464
(212) 885-0701, Founded 1976.

The Brooklyn Children's Museum
145 Brooklyn Ave.
Brooklyn, NY 11213
(718) 735-4400, Founded 1899.

★ **Buffalo Museum of Science**
1020 Humboldt Pkwy.
Buffalo, NY 14211
(716) 896-5200, Founded 1861.

**Vanderbilt Museum: Mansion,
Marine Museum, Planetarium**
180 Little Neck Rd., P.O. Box F
Centerport, NY 11721
(516) 262-7880, Founded 1950.

★ **Museums of the Hudson Highlands**
The Boulevard, P.O. Box 181
Cornwall-on-the-Hudson, NY 12520
(914) 534-7781, Founded 1962.

Science Museum
State University Science Building
Bowers Hall
Cortland, NY 13045
(607) 753-2715, Founded 1964.

★ **Trailside Nature Museum**
Ward Pound Ridge Reservation
Cross River, NY 10518
(914) 763-3993, Founded 1937.

Alley Pond Environmental Center, Inc.
228-06 Northern Blvd.
Douglaston, NY 11363
(718) 229-4000, Founded 1976.

Durham Center Museum, Inc.
Star Route 1, P.O. Box 28
East Durham, NY 12423
(518) 239-8461, Founded 1960.

★ **Pember Museum of Natural History**
33 W. Main St.
Granville, NY 12832
(518) 642-1515, Founded 1909.

Bayard Cutting Arboretum
Montauk Highway
Great River, NY 11739
(516) 581-1002, Founded 1952.

**The Gregory Museum: Long Island
Earth Science Center**
Heitz Place
Hicksville, NY 11801
(516) 822-7505, Founded 1963.

Remington Gun Museum
Catherine Street
Ilion, NY 13357
(315) 894-9961, Founded 1959.

L. H. Bailey Hortorium
Cornell University
Ithaca, NY 14853
(607) 255-2131, Founded 1935.

★ **Paleontological Research Institution**
1259 Trumansburg Rd.
Ithaca, NY 14850
(607) 273-6623, Founded 1932.

**Lake George Historical
Association Museum**
Canada Street
Lake George, NY 12845
(518) 668-5044, Founded 1964.

Lake Placid-North Elba Historical Society
Averyville Road
Lake Placid, NY 12946
(518) 523-1608, Founded 1961.

Science Museum of Long Island
Leeds Pond Preserve
1526 North Plandome Rd.
Manhasset , NY 11030
(516) 627-9400, Founded 1963.

Museum Village in Orange County
Museum Village Road
Monroe, NY 10950
(914) 782-8247, Founded 1950.

Westmoreland Sanctuary, Inc.
Chestnut Ridge Road
Mount Kisco, NY 10549
(914) 666-8448, Founded 1957.

Mohonk Preserve, Inc.
Mohonk Lake
New Paltz, NY 12561
(914) 255-0919, Founded 1963.

★ **American Museum of Natural History**
Central Park West at 79th St.
New York, NY 10024
(212) 769-5000, Founded 1869.

Central Park Learning Center Belvedere Castle
Central Park Conservancy, The Arsenal
830 5th Ave.
New York, NY 10021
(212) 772-0210

★ **Museum of Natural History**
Quaker Hill
Pawling, NY 12564
(914) 855-5099, Founded 1960.

★ **Petrified Creatures Museum
of Natural History**
Road 2, Route 20
Richfield Springs, NY 13439
(315) 858-2868, Founded 1934.

★ **Rochester Museum and Science Center**
657 East Ave., P.O. Box 1480
Rochester, NY 14603-1480
(716) 271-4320, Founded 1912.

The Greenburgh Nature Center
Dromore Road
Scarsdale, NY 10583
(914) 723-3470, Founded 1975.

Schenectady Museum and Planetarium
Nott Terrace Heights
Schenectady, NY 12308
(518) 382-7890, Founded 1934.

Staten Island Institute of Arts and Sciences
75 Stuyvesant Place
Staten Island, NY 10301
(718) 727-1135, Founded 1881.

★ **Museum of Long Island Natural Sciences**
Earth and Space Sciences Building
State University of New York at Stony Brook
Stony Brook, NY 11794
(516) 632-8230, Founded 1973.

Rensselaer County Junior Museum
282 5th Ave.
Troy, NY 12182
(518) 235-2120, Founded 1954.

Children's Museum of History
Natural History and Science at Utica, New York
311 Main St.
Utica, NY 13501
(315) 724-6128, Founded 1963.

Sci–Tech Center of Northern New York
317 Washington St., N.Y.S. Office Building
Watertown, NY 13601
(315) 788-1340, Founded 1982.

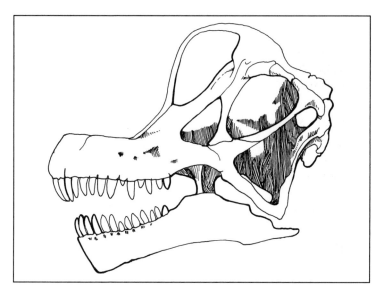

Skull of *Brachiosaurus*, called "arm lizard."

NORTH CAROLINA

Morrow Mountain State Park
Morrow Mountain Road
Albermarle, NC 28001
(704) 982-4402, Founded 1962.

★ **Colburn Gem and Mineral Museum, Inc.**
Civic Center Complex
Haywood Street
Asheville, NC 28801
(704) 254-7162, Founded 1960.

★ **North Carolina Maritime Museum**
315 Front St.
Beaufort, NC 28516
(919) 728-7317, Founded 1975.

Hatteras Island Visitor Center
Buxton, NC 27920
(919) 473-2111, Founded 1953.

Discovery Place
301 N. Tryon St.
Charlotte, NC 28202
(704) 372-6262, Founded 1981.

★ **Nature Museum**
1658 Sterling Rd.
Charlotte, NC 28209
(704) 372-6261, Founded 1947.

North Carolina Museum of Life and Science
433 Murray Ave.
Durham , NC 27704
(919) 477-0431, Founded 1946.

★ **Schiele Museum of Natural History
and Planetarium, Inc.**
1500 E. Garrison Blvd.
Gastonia, NC 28053
(704) 866-6900, Founded 1960.

★ **The Natural Science Center
of Greensboro, Inc.**
4301 Lawndale Dr.
Greensboro, NC 27408
(919) 288-3769, Founded 1957.

Catawba Science Center
243 3rd Ave. NE
Hickory, NC 28601
(704) 322-8169, Founded 1972.

**Piedmont Environmental Education
Center of High Point**
1228 Penny Road
High Point, NC 27260
(919) 454-4214, Founded 1973.

Lake Waccamaw Depot Museum
Flemington Drive
Lake Waccamaw, NC 28450
(919) 646-3918, Founded 1977.

Davidson County Historical Museum
2 S. Main St., Oakwood House
Lexington, NC 27292
(704) 249-7011, Founded 1976.

Ocracoke Island Visitor Center
Ocracoke, NC 27960
(919) 473-2111, Founded 1956.

★ **North Carolina State Museum of Natural Science**
102 N Salisbury St.
Raleigh, NC 27611
(919) 733-7450, Founded 1877.

Onslow County Museum
102 Hargett St.
Richlands, NC 28574
(919) 324-5008, Founded 1976.

★ **Horizons Unlimited**
Supplementary Education Center
1636 Parkview Circle
Salisbury, NC 28144
(704) 636-3462, Founded 1967.

Cliffs of the Neuse State Park
Route 2, P.O. Box 50
Seven Springs, NC 28578
(919) 778-6234, Founded 1979.

Bodie Island Visitor Center
Bodie Island Lighthouse
South Nags Head, NC 27959
(919) 473-2111, Founded 1956.

★ **Weymouth Woods-Sandhills**
Nature Preserve Museums
400 N. Fort Bragg Rd.
Southern Pines, NC 28387
(919) 692-2167, Founded 1969.

★ **New Hanover County Museum**
of the Lower Cape Fear
814 Market St.
Wilmington, NC 28401
(919) 341-4350, Founded 1898.

Nature Science Center
Museum Drive
Winston-Salem, NC 27105
(919) 767-6730, Founded 1964.

Anchisaurus skeleton from the Triassic period.

OHIO

★ **Ehrhart Museum**
City Hall
North Main Street
Antwerp, OH 45813
(419) 258-8161, Founded 1963.

Lake Erie Nature and Science Center
28728 Wolf Rd.
Bay Village, OH 44140
(216) 871-2900, Founded 1945.

★ **Cincinnati Museum of Natural
History and Planetarium**
1720 Gilbert Ave.
Cincinnati, OH 45202
(513) 621-3889, Founded 1835.

Trailside Nature Center and Museum
Brookline Drive
Burnet Woods Park
Cincinnati, OH 45220
(513) 751-3679, Founded 1930.

★ **Cleveland Museum of Natural History**
Wade Oval
University Circle
Cleveland, OH 44106
(216) 231-4600, Founded 1920.

**Columbiana and Fairfield Township
Historical Society**
12 E. Park Ave.
Columbiana, OH 44408
(216) 482-4408, Founded 1953.

Ohio Historical Center
Interstate 71 and 17th Ave.
Columbus, OH 43211
(614) 297-2300, Founded 1885.

**Orton Geological Museum,
Ohio State University**
155 S. Oval Mall
Columbus, OH 43210
(614) 292-4473, Founded 1892.

Aullwood Audubon Center and Farm
1000 Aullwood Rd.
Dayton, OH 45414
(513) 890-7360, Founded 1957.

★ **Dayton Museum of Natural History**
2629 Ridge Ave.
Dayton, OH 45414
(513) 275-7431, Founded 1893.

Au Glaize Village
Krouse Road
Defiance, OH 43512
(419) 784-0107, Founded 1966.

★ **Flint Ridge State Memorial Museum**
7091 Brownsville Rd. SE
Glenford, OH 43739
(614) 787-2476, Founded 1933.

Granville Historical Museum
115 E. Broadway
Granville, OH 43023
(614) 587-3951, Founded 1885.

Fort Hill Museum
13614 Fort Hill Rd.
Hillsboro, OH 45133
(513) 588-3221

**Sullivan-Johnson Museum
of Hardin County**
223 N. Main St.
Kenton, OH 43326
(419) 673-7147, Founded 1984.

**Warren County Historical
Society Museum**
105 S. Broadway, P.O. Box 223
Lebanon, OH 45036
(513) 932-1817, Founded 1940.

Allen County Museum
620 W. Market St.
Lima, OH 45801
(419) 222-9426, Founded 1908.

Milan Historical Museum, Inc.
10 Edison Dr.
Milan, OH 44846
(419) 499-2968, Founded 1929.

Firelands Historical Society Museum
4 Case Ave.
Norwalk, OH 44857
(419) 668-6038, Founded 1857.

★ **Toledo Museum of Natural Sciences**
2700 Broadway
Toledo, OH 43609
(419) 385-5721, Founded 1938.

The Wilderness Center Inc.
9877 Alabama Ave. SW
Wilmot, OH 44689
(216) 359-5235, Founded 1964.

Wayne County Historical Society
546 E. Bowman St.
Wooster, OH 44691
(216) 264-8856, Founded 1954.

★ **Trailside Museum**
505 Corry St.
Yellow Springs, OH 45387
(513) 767-7798, Founded 1951.

Ford Nature Education Center
840 Old Furnace Rd.
Youngstown, OH 44511
(216) 740-7107, Founded 1972.

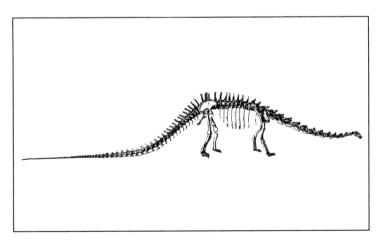

Diplodocus skeleton from the Jurassic period.

PENNSYLVANIA

Tioga Point Museum
724 S. Main St.
Athens, PA 18810
(717) 888-7225, Founded 1895.

Lehigh University Art Galleries
Chandler–Ullman Hall #17
Bethlehem, PA 18015
(215) 758-3615, Founded 1864.

Riverbend Environmental Education Center
P.O. Box 2, Spring Mill Road
Gladwyne, PA 19035
(215) 527-5234, Founded 1974.

The State Museum of Pennsylvania
3rd and North Streets
Harrisburg, PA 17108
(717) 787-4980, Founded 1905.

Gilman Museum at the Cave
Hellertown, PA 18055
(215) 838-8767, Founded 1955.

**The North Museum of Franklin
and Marshall College**
College and Buchanan Avenues
Lancaster, PA 17604
(717) 291-3941, Founded 1901.

★ **Academy of Natural Sciences
of Philadelphia**
19th and The Parkway
Philadelphia, PA 19103
(215) 299-1000, Founded 1812.

**The Schnylkill Center
for the Environmental Education**
8480 Hagy's Mill Rd.
Philadelphia, PA 19128
(215) 482-7300, Founded 1965.

★ **Wagner Free Institute of Science**
17th St. and Montgomery Avenue
Philadelphia, PA 19121
(215) 763-6529, Founded 1855.

★ **The Carnegie Museum of Natural History**
4400 Forbes Ave.
Pittsburgh, PA 15213
(412) 622-3243, Founded 1896.

Reading Public Museum and Art Gallery
500 Museum Rd.
Reading, PA 19611-1425
(215) 371-5850, Founded 1904.

★ **Everhart Museum**
Nay Aug Park
Scranton, PA 18510
(717) 346-7186, Founded 1908.

★ **The Frost Entomological Museum,
The Pennsylvania State University**
Patterson Building, Department of Entomology
University Park, PA 16802
(814) 863-1863, Founded 1968.

Lycoming County Historical Museum
858 W. 4th St.
Williamsport, PA 17701
(717) 326-3326, Founded 1865.

RHODE ISLAND

★ **Roger Williams Park Museum of Natural History**
Roger Williams Park
Providence, RI 02905
(401) 785-9450, Founded 1896.

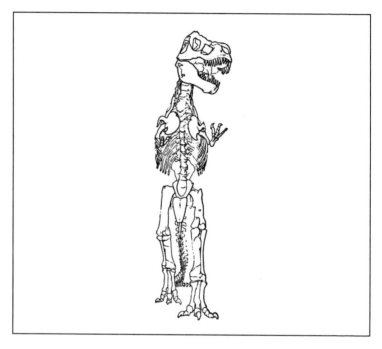

The carnivorous dinosaur *Tyrannosaurus rex* from the Cretaceous
period.

SOUTH CAROLINA

Beaufort Museum
713 Cravens St.
Beaufort, SC 29901
(803) 525-7471, Founded 1939.

Charles Towne Landing-1670
1500 Old Town Rd.
Charleston, SC 29407
(803) 556-4450, Founded 1970.

The Charleston Museum
360 Meeting St.
Charleston, SC 29403
(803) 722-2996, Founded 1773.

South Carolina State Museum
301 Gervais St.
Columbia, SC 29201
(803) 737-4921, Founded 1973.

The Museum
106 Main St.
Greenwood, SC 29646
(803) 229-7093, Founded 1968.

Myrtle Beach State Park Nature Center
Highway 17 South
Myrtle Beach, SC 29577
(803) 238-5325, Founded 1970.

Museum of York County
4621 Mount Gallant Rd.
Rock Hill, SC 29732
(803) 329-2121, Founded 1950.

★ **Spartanburg County Nature-Science Center**
385 S. Spring St.
Spartanburg, SC 29301
(803) 583-2777, Founded 1978.

TENNESSEE

Chattanooga Nature Center
400 Garden Rd.
Chattanooga, TN 37419
(615) 821-1160, Founded 1978.

Sugarlands Visitors Center
Great Smoky Mountains National Park
Gatlinburg, TN 37738
(615) 436-1290, Founded 1961.

Frank H. McClung Museum
University of Tennessee
Circle Park Drive
Knoxville, TN 37996
(615) 974-2144, Founded 1961.

Lichterman Nature Center
5992 Quince Rd.
Memphis, TN 38119
(901) 767-7322, Founded 1983.

★ **Memphis Pink Palace Museum and Planetarium**
3050 Central Ave.
Memphis, TN 38111
(901) 454-5600, Founded 1928.

Mississippi River Museum at Mud Island
125 N. Front St.
Memphis, TN 38103
(901) 576-7230, Founded 1978.

★ **Cumberland Science Museum**
800 Ridley Blvd.
Nashville, TN 37203
(615) 259-6099, Founded 1944.

Grassmere Wildlife Park
3777 Nolensville Rd.
Nashville, TN 37211
(615) 833-1534, Founded 1990.

Children's Museum of Oak Ridge, Inc.
461 W. Outer Dr.
Oak Ridge, TN 37830
(615) 482-1074, Founded 1973.

VERMONT

Discovery Museum
51 Park St.
Essex Junction, VT 05452
(802) 878-8687, Founded 1974.

Montshire Museum of Science, Inc.
Montshire Road
Norwich, VT 05055
(802) 649-2200, Founded 1975.

Fairbanks Museum and Planetarium
Main and Prospect Streets
St. Johnsbury, VT 05819
(802) 748-2372, Founded 1889.

Shelburne Museum, Inc.
U.S. Route 7
Shelburne, VT 05482
(802) 985-3346, Founded 1947.

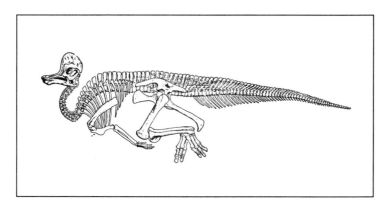

Corythosaurus skeleton from the Cretaceous period.

VIRGINIA

Ramsay Nature Center
5700 Sanger Ave.
Alexandria, VA 22311
(703) 838-4829, Founded 1979.

Bedford City/County Museum
201 E. Main St.
Bedford, VA 24323
(703) 586-4520, Founded 1932.

★ **Peaks of Otter Visitor Center**
RFD 2, Box 163
Bedford, VA 24523
(703) 586-4357

Southwest Virginia Museum
10 W. 1st St.
Big Stone Gap, VA 24219
(703) 523-1322, Founded 1943.

Museum of the Geological Sciences
Virginia Polytechnic Institute and
State University
Derring Hall
Blacksburg, VA 24061
(703) 231-6029, Founded 1969.

**Walney Visitor Center-
At Ellanor C. Lawrence Park**
5040 Walney Road
Chantilly, VA 22021
(703) 631-0013, Founded 1971.

Chesterfield County Museum
Chesterfield Courthouse Square
Chesterfield, VA 23832
(804) 748-1026, Founded 1961.

★ **Oyster Museum of Chinco**
Beach Road
Chincoteague, VA 23336
(804) 336-6117, Founded 1966.

Jeff Matthews Memorial Museum
606 W. Stuart Drive
Galax, VA 24333
(703) 236-7874, Founded 1974.

★ **D. Ralph Hostetter Museum**
of Natural History
Eastern Mennonite College
Harrisonburg, VA 22801
(703) 433-2771, Founded 1968.

Shenandoah National Park
Luray, VA 22835
(703) 999-2243, Founded 1935.

★ **Virginia Museum**
of Natural History
1001 Douglas Ave.
Martinsville, VA 24112
(703) 666-8600, Founded 1984.

Virginia Living Museum
524 J. Clyde Morris Blvd.
Newport News, Va 23601
(804) 595-1900, Founded 1964.

Virginia Zoological Park
3500 Granby St.
Norfolk, VA 23504
(804) 441-5227, Founded 1907.

★ **Lora Robins Gallery of Design from Nature**
University of Richmond
Richmond, VA 23173
(804) 289-8460, Founded 1977.

Science Museum of Western Virginia
1 Market Square
Roanoke, VA 24011
(703) 342-5710, Founded 1970.

Prince William Forest Park
Route 619
Triangle, VA 22172
(703) 221-2104, Founded 1947.

Seashore State Park
Natural Area Visitor Center
2500 Shore Dr.
Virginia Beach, VA 23451
(804) 481-4836, Founded 1936.

Virginia Marine Science Museum
717 General Booth Blvd.
Virginia Beach, VA 23451
(804) 425-3474

WEST VIRGINIA

Sunrise Museums, Inc.
746 Myrtle Rd.
Charleston, WV 25314
(304) 344-8035, Founded 1961.

Geology Museum
Marshall University
3rd Ave. and Hal Greer Blvd.
Huntington, WV 25755
(304) 696-6720, Founded 1837.

WISCONSIN

Ridges Sanctuary
8288 Highway Q
Baileys Harbor, WI 54202
(414) 839-2802, Founded 1937.

International Crane Foundation
East 11376 Shady Lane Rd.
Baraboo, WI 53913-9778
(608) 356-9462, Founded 1973.

Apostles Islands National Lakeshore
415 W. Washington Ave.
Bayfield, WI 54814
(715) 779-3397, Founded 1970.

Dodge County Historical Society Museum
105 Park Ave.
Beaver Dam, WI 53916
(414) 887-1266, Founded 1938.

★ **Cable Natural History Museum Inc.**
County Highway M and Randysek Road
Cable, WI 54821
(715) 798-3890, Founded 1968.

Peninsula State Park
Shore Road
Fish Creek, WI 54212
(414) 868-3258

Galloway House and Village
336 Old Pioneer Rd.
Fond Du Lac, WI 54935
(414) 922-6390, Founded 1955.

Neville Public Museum of Brown County
210 Museum Pl.
Green Bay, WI 54303
(414) 436-3767, Founded 1915.

**National Fresh Water Fishing
Hall of Fame**
Hall of Fame Drive
Hayward, WI 54843
(715) 634-4440, Founded 1960.

★ **Kenosha Public Museum**
5608 10th Ave.
Kenosha, WI 53140
(414) 656-8026, Founded 1933.

University of Wisconsin Arboretum-Madison
1207 Seminole Highway
Madison, WI 53711
(608) 263-7888, Founded 1934.

University of Wisconsin Zoological Museum
Lowell Noland Building
Madison, WI 53706
(608) 262-3766, Founded 1887.

Thunderbird Museum
Hatfield Route 1
Merrillan, WI 54754
(715) 333-5841, Founded 1959.

**Greene Memorial Museum,
University of Wisconsin-Milwaukee**
3367 N. Downer Ave.
Milwaukee, WI 53211
(414) 229-4794, Founded 1913.

Milwaukee Public Museum
800 W. Wells St.
Milwaukee, WI 53233
(414) 278-2702, Founded 1882.

New London Public Museum
412 S. Pearl St.
New London, WI 54961
(414) 982-8520, Founded 1932

Oshkosh Public Museum
1331 Algoma Blvd.
Oshkosh, WI 54901
(414) 236-5150, Founded 1911.

Rollo Jamison Museum
405 E. Main St.
Platteville, WI 53818
(608) 348-3301, Founded 1981.

★ **Mackenzie Environmental Education Center**
Route 2, P.O. Box 825
Poynette, WI 53955
(608) 635-4498, Founded 1961.

The House on the Rock
Route 3
Spring Green, WI 53588
(608) 935-3639, Founded 1961.

★ **The Museum of Natural History**
900 Reserve St.
University of Wisconsin
Stevens Point, WI 54481
(715) 346-2858, Founded 1966.

Waukesha County Historical Museum
101 W. Main St.
Waukesha, WI 53186
(414) 548-7186, Founded 1914.

TIME PERIODS

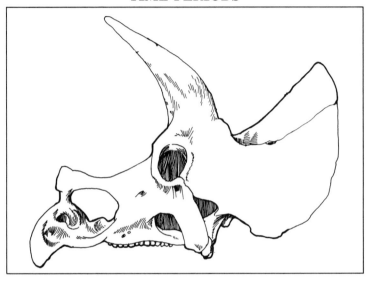

Permian period, 280-225 million years ago.
Triassic period, 225-195 million years ago.
Jurassic period, 195-136 million years ago.
Cretaceous period, 136-65 million years ago.
Tertiary period, 65-3 million years ago.
Quaternary period, 3 million years ago to present.

WHY JOIN
A MUSEUM?

Among the many reasons patrons become museum members are free or reduced admissions, subscriptions to a newsletter or magazine, and enhanced volunteer opportunities. Some offer other benefits such as special programs, workshops, and seminars. A private members-only lounge or study room may be another bonus. Some membership benefits are honored at other organizations. Also important are tour and travel possibilities, early exhibit previews, and social events. Behind the scene tours and free parking and garment checking are also possible. Some group insurance opportunities exist, along with museum store discounts. And let's not forget the tax deduction.

Discounts are not the only reason for becoming a member. Patrons often join because museums provide a stability and a permanence in changing landscapes. They also join because museums can offer a source of local pride. Some even seek an immortality with having their name listed in civic works and the social status that goes along with it. You can also simply donate for the love of the exhibits. Most museums offer some or all of these benefits. Whatever your reasons may be, our museums need our support—and we certainly need them.

RECOMMENDED READING

Alexander, Edward P. *Museum Masters*. Nashville: American Association for State and Local History, 1983.

Cutchins, Judy. *Are Those Animals Real?* New York: William Morrow and Company, Inc., 1984.

Danilov, Victor J. *Science and Technology Centers*. Massachusettes Institute of Technology, 1982.

Gurney, Gene. *The Smithsonian Institution*. New York: Crown Publishers, Inc., 1964.

Hoffman, Paul. *American Museum Guides*. New York: Macmillan Publishing Company, Inc., 1983.

Kopper, Philip. *The National Museum of Natural History.* New York: Harry N. Abrams Inc., Publishers, 1982.

Papajani, Janet. *Museums.* Regensteiner Publishing Enterprises, Inc., 1983.

Preston, Douglas J. *Dinosaurs in the Attic.* New York: Random House, Inc., 1986.

Ross, Richard. *Museology.* Aperature Foundation, Inc., 1989.

Thomson, Peggy. *Auks, Rocks and the Odd Dinosaur.* New York: Thomas Y. Crowell Junior Books, 1985.

INDEX BY STATE

A WONDERFUL GIFT FOR YOUR MUSEUM-LOVING FRIENDS AND RELATIVES!

ORDER FORM

YES, I want _____ copies of *Natural History Museums, Volume I* at $12.95 each, plus $3 shipping per book. (Florida residents, please add 78¢ sales tax.) Canadian orders must be accompanied by a postal money order in U.S. funds. Allow 30 days for delivery.

____Check or money order enclosed

Name _____ Phone _____

Address _____

City/State/Zip _____

Check your leading bookstore.

Please make your check payable and return to:

**Batax Museum Publishing
301 Racquet Club Road, Suite 202
Fort Lauderdale, FL 33326**

Write for information on Volume II,
Natural History Museums in the Western United States